INSIDE THE
NFL

NEW YORK
JETS

BY TODD RYAN

SportsZone

An Imprint of Abdo Publishing
abdobooks.com

abdobooks.com

Published by Abdo Publishing, a division of ABDO, PO Box 398166, Minneapolis, Minnesota 55439. Copyright © 2020 by Abdo Consulting Group, Inc. International copyrights reserved in all countries. No part of this book may be reproduced in any form without written permission from the publisher. SportsZone™ is a trademark and logo of Abdo Publishing.

Printed in the United States of America, North Mankato, Minnesota
042019
092019

Cover Photo: Lynne Sladky/AP Images
Interior Photos: Focus on Sport/Getty Images Sport/Getty Images, 4, 25; Focus on Sport/ Getty Images, 7; NFL Photos/AP Images, 9; Bettmann/Getty Images, 11; AP Images, 13, 15, 19, 43; Tony Tomsic/AP Images, 20; Paul Spinelli/AP Images, 27; Al Messerschmidt/AP Images, 29, 35; Bill Kostroun/AP Images, 31; Tom DiPace/AP Images, 36; Denis Poroy/AP Images, 38; Damian Strohmeyer/AP Images, 41

Editor: Patrick Donnelly
Series Designer: Craig Hinton

Library of Congress Control Number: 2018965644

Publisher's Cataloging-in-Publication Data

Names: Ryan, Todd, author.
Title: New York Jets / by Todd Ryan
Description: Minneapolis, Minnesota: Abdo Publishing, 2020 | Series: Inside the NFL | Includes online resources and index.
Identifiers: ISBN 9781532118609 (lib. bdg.) | ISBN 9781532172786 (ebook)
Subjects: LCSH: New York Jets (Football team)--Juvenile literature. | National Football League--Juvenile literature. | Football teams--Juvenile literature. | American football--Juvenile literature.
Classification: DDC 796.33264--dc23

TABLE OF
CONTENTS

CHAPTER 1

THE GUARANTEE

The first two Super Bowls showed that American Football League (AFL) teams were not quite ready to defeat their National Football League (NFL) rivals. Joe Namath, however, guaranteed that things were about to change.

In 1968 Namath's New York Jets won the championship of the AFL, a league that began play in 1960 as a rival to the NFL. The Jets were set to play the NFL-champion Baltimore Colts in Super Bowl III on January 12, 1969, in Miami. In the two weeks leading up to the big game, the constant talk was about how the Colts were simply too strong for the Jets. On the Thursday night before Super Bowl Sunday, the Miami Touchdown Club presented Namath an award. As Namath headed to the front of the room to accept the award, a fan heckled him about how much stronger the Colts were. The remarks drew laughter from the audience.

Joe Namath drops back to pass against the Baltimore Colts during Super Bowl III.

The 25-year-old quarterback told the crowd he was tired of hearing about it. He did not stop there. "We're gonna win the game," Namath said. "I guarantee it." After that, there was little else to talk about besides Namath's bold prediction until the Super Bowl was played.

The Colts were favored by nearly three touchdowns, and with good reason. First, Baltimore was from the NFL. That league had been around much longer than the AFL. It had also produced the first two Super Bowl winners. The Green Bay Packers easily dispatched the Kansas City Chiefs in Super Bowl I and did the same to the Oakland Raiders in Super Bowl II.

The Colts also had a record of 13–1 in what was believed to be the tougher league. The Jets went 11–3 in the AFL. In the NFL Championship Game, Baltimore hammered the Cleveland Browns 34–0. The Jets

DON MAYNARD

The AFL came around just in time for Don Maynard. The former Texas Western College star lasted just one season in the NFL after being drafted by the New York Giants. The wide receiver played in the Canadian Football League in 1959 before becoming an original member of the New York Titans in 1960. The Titans would later change their name to the Jets. Maynard succeeded right away in the AFL. He later clicked with quarterback Joe Namath. Both went on to be inducted into the Pro Football Hall of Fame. Through 2018 Maynard still held the Jets' all-time records with 627 receptions, 11,732 receiving yards, and 88 touchdown catches.

✗ Jets running back Matt Snell (41) powers over the goal line for a touchdown in Super Bowl III.

had to rally in the fourth quarter to slip past the Raiders 27–23 in the AFL Championship Game. The NFL's top-ranked defense figured to be too strong for the offense run by Namath.

Namath was flashy. Old-school football types considered "Broadway Joe" to be all style and no substance. But the Jets attacked the Colts without much flash from Namath. They stuck to a solid, basic game plan as they tried to pull off one of the greatest upsets in pro football history.

The New York defense held Baltimore scoreless in the first half. Namath passed well. But running back Matt Snell was just as important. His 4-yard touchdown run in the second quarter gave the Jets a 7–0 halftime lead. In the second half, Jets kicker Jim Turner booted three field goals, pushing the lead to a shocking 16–0.

When it came time to protect that lead in the fourth quarter, Namath did not throw a pass. The Jets used their ground game to take time off the clock and closed out a 16–7 victory. Namath finished 17-for-28 passing for 206 yards. He also was given credit for changing many plays at the line of scrimmage. This countered Baltimore's aggressive defense.

On the biggest day of his career and in Jets history, Namath was selected as the Most Valuable Player (MVP) of the Super Bowl. The Super Bowl began in 1966 when the NFL and AFL agreed to merge into one larger league. There was uncertainty, though, whether the combined league would create even competition. And there were concerns about whether the Super Bowl would develop the popularity worthy of a championship game. Namath's guarantee gave more people a reason to watch the game. The Jets' win gave people more reason to watch professional football in the future.

✕ Namath tells the world the Jets are No. 1 as he runs off the Orange Bowl field after defeating the Colts.

By the time the 1970 season started, a little more than a year and a half after Super Bowl III, the AFL was gone. It had become part of the NFL. With help from Namath and the Jets, the new NFL was on its way to becoming the most popular pro sports league in the United States.

CHAPTER 2

TAKING OFF

New York City was awarded one of the original franchises when the AFL was formed on August 14, 1959. The team was named the New York Titans and would play its home games at the Polo Grounds when the AFL kicked off its inaugural season in 1960.

By 1962 the Titans were losing on the field and struggling in attendance. After two 7–7 seasons under their first head coach, former NFL star Sammy Baugh, they went just 5–9 in 1962. Before their third season was over, the Titans were in danger of extinction.

Owner Harry Wismer was losing so much money that he was unable to pay his players and team employees. The AFL took over the costs of running the bankrupt operation from November 8 to the end of the 1962 season.

Titans head coach Sammy Baugh runs a Titans practice at New York's Polo Grounds in 1960.

The New York Titans defeated the Buffalo Bills 27–3 in their first game on September 11, 1960. The Titans finished their first season 7–7. Don Maynard caught 72 passes to lead the team. Maynard and Art Powell were the first professional wide receiver teammates to each post 1,000 receiving yards in the same season.

The team's name, the Titans, was gone before the 1963 season. But the team remained. David A. "Sonny" Werblin led a five-man group that purchased the team for $1 million on March 28, 1963.

On April 15, the new owners named Weeb Ewbank as their head coach and general manager. Ewbank had formerly been the Baltimore Colts' head coach. The new owners also changed the team's name from Titans to Jets. The team was planning to move to new Shea Stadium in the borough of Queens. It was located between New York's two biggest airports, making the name "Jets" appropriate.

The results on the field changed little, however. The Jets went 5–8–1 in each of their first three seasons with the new nickname and ownership. Positive changes were starting to occur, though.

The Jets whipped the Denver Broncos 30–6 in their Shea Stadium debut on September 12, 1964. The talent level of the Jets' players was on the rise. After each of the first two

✖ The Jets moved into brand-new Shea Stadium in 1964.

seasons under new ownership, the Jets drafted and signed the eventual AFL Rookie of the Year, running back Matt Snell and quarterback Joe Namath.

Through 1966 the AFL and NFL held separate drafts. The best players were usually drafted by a team from each league,

JOE NAMATH

Joe Namath brought excitement to professional football. Namath was nicknamed "Broadway Joe" for the attention he received while enjoying the New York City nightlife. On the field, Namath was best known for two things. The first was the Super Bowl III upset victory that he guaranteed and delivered. The second was his battle with knee injuries.

Namath was the AFL Rookie of the Year in 1965. He led the Jets to their first Eastern Division and AFL championships in 1968. He followed them up with the 16–7 Super Bowl win over the Baltimore Colts in January 1969. He was the AFL Player of the Year in the championship season, which he capped as MVP of the Super Bowl.

Namath threw for 27,663 yards and 173 touchdowns in 12 seasons with the Jets and a final season with the Los Angeles Rams in 1977.

and those teams often had bidding wars as they tried to convince the players to sign with them.

The Jets chose Snell with their first pick in the 1964 AFL Draft. The fullback from Ohio State University was also selected by New York's NFL team, the Giants, but he signed with the Jets. His signing marked the first time the Titans/Jets franchise was able to sign its first-round draft pick. Snell was named second-team all-AFL in his rookie season after rushing for 948 yards and catching 56 passes.

✗ Jets coach/general manager Weeb Ewbank, *left*, and owner Sonny Werblin are all smiles as quarterback Joe Namath signs with the team on January 2, 1965.

But the Jets were not finished. On January 2, 1965, they signed Namath, one day after Namath's unbeaten University of Alabama team had fallen 21–17 to the University of Texas in the Orange Bowl. The St. Louis Cardinals had chosen Namath with the twelfth pick of the NFL Draft in November 1964. The Jets selected Namath with the first overall pick of the AFL Draft on the same day. New York won the bidding war for his services

THE HEIDI GAME

The Jets lost just once in their final 11 games during the 1968 season. That loss came against the Oakland Raiders in one of pro football's most infamous games. It was notorious for NBC-TV's decision to cut off its live broadcast with 50 seconds left in the game. The Jets had kicked a field goal to take a 32–29 lead just 15 seconds earlier. With the outcome still undecided, NBC kept to its advertised schedule. It aired the children's movie *Heidi* at 7:00 p.m. The broadcast ended, but the Raiders did not stop playing. They scored twice in the last 42 seconds for a 43–32 victory. After enraged fans flooded the NBC switchboard with angry calls, the NFL changed its broadcast policy to ensure that all games would be shown in their entirety in the markets of the teams playing.

with a contract worth a reported $427,000, the largest ever signed by a pro football player at the time.

Namath had injured his knee during his senior year at Alabama. He underwent knee surgery in New York within a month of signing with the Jets. It was the first of many surgeries that would mar an otherwise outstanding career.

Namath made his pro debut starting the Jets' second game in 1965. He completed less than half of his passes that rookie season. However, he did throw for 2,220 yards and 18 touchdowns.

The Jets started showing improvement with Namath running the offense. The 1966 team started out 4–0–1, only to slip to a 6–6–2 final record. A loss in the 1967 opener was followed by a six-game unbeaten streak to propel the Jets to 5–1–1. By Thanksgiving, the team had clinched its first winning season.

Namath threw for 343 yards in a season-ending 42–31 victory over the San Diego Chargers as the Jets finished 8–5–1. Namath became the first professional quarterback to pass for more than 4,000 yards in a season, with 4,007.

The Jets began their 1968 season 3–2 before getting on a roll. They won eight of their last nine games to finish 11–3. That was good enough for first place in the Eastern Division, giving them a spot in the AFL Championship Game at Shea Stadium against the West champion Oakland Raiders.

In the fourth quarter, the Raiders scored 10 straight points to take a 23–20 lead. However, Namath connected with Don Maynard on a 6-yard touchdown pass, and the Jets held on to win 27–23. New York then went on to record its historic win over the Baltimore Colts in Super Bowl III. It was one of the defining moments for the franchise and for professional football.

CHAPTER 3

JOINING THE NFL

The NFL and AFL played one more season as separate leagues after the Jets won Super Bowl III. The 1969 Jets went 10–4 to repeat as Eastern Division champions. However, they lost to the Kansas City Chiefs 13–6 in the AFL semifinals.

For the 1970 season, all of the old AFL teams stayed together in the American Football Conference (AFC). The Jets were placed in the East, one of three divisions in the AFC. The Jets, Boston Patriots, Buffalo Bills, and Miami Dolphins stayed together. They were joined by the Baltimore Colts, who moved over from the old NFL. The division rivals would face each other twice every season.

The Jets had returned to the playoffs the season after they won the Super Bowl. But they soon entered an

Joe Namath and the Jets had more than their share of tough times after joining the NFL in 1970.

× The Jets and Cleveland Browns played in the first *Monday Night Football* game on ABC-TV.

extended dry spell. Namath and the team showed occasional flashes of brilliance. But the quarterback's injuries forced him out of the lineup for long periods. He sometimes played poorly when he returned.

In their fifth game as NFL members, the Jets faced the Baltimore Colts for the first time since Super Bowl III. Namath suffered a broken right wrist but made it through the 29–22 loss. However, he did not play again the rest of the season. The Jets ended their first year in the NFL with a 4–10 record.

Namath missed more than a year of regular-season action. After recovering from the wrist injury, he injured his left knee while trying to make a tackle on a fumble return in a 1971 preseason game. The injury required surgery. Namath didn't return to the field until the eleventh game of the 1971 season.

The best two seasons the Jets could produce with Namath in the NFL were 1972 and 1974. Even then, the Jets went 7–7 in both years.

The team's biggest offensive stars of the 1970s each had their moments in the 1972 season. Namath got the show started on September 24 when he and the Jets beat the Colts and Johnny Unitas in a 44–34 victory. The teams set what was

END OF AN ERA

Joe Namath finished his career by playing four games with the Los Angeles Rams in 1977. After Namath played for the Jets from 1965 through 1976, the team tried to honor his request for a trade to the Rams. When a trade could not be completed, the Jets released Namath. This made him free to sign with Los Angeles. Namath played in two wins and two losses with the Rams. He then retired when the season was over.

then a league record by combining for 872 passing yards. Namath threw for 496 yards and six touchdowns.

The backfield combination of John Riggins and Emerson Boozer starred on October 15. Riggins ran for 168 yards and Boozer 150 more in a 41–13 rout of the Patriots. The Jets totaled a team-record 333 rushing yards.

Don Maynard passed Raymond Berry and became professional football's all-time leader in receptions. Maynard made career catch number 632 during a 24–16 loss to the Oakland Raiders on *Monday Night Football* on December 11.

The Jets were on the wrong end of a record-setting day the next year. Weeb Ewbank's coaching career came to an end on December 16, 1973. The Bills pounded the Jets 34–14 at Shea Stadium. O. J. Simpson ran for 200 yards. That gave him 2,003 rushing yards for the year and made him the first runner in pro football history to top 2,000 rushing yards in a season.

While the 7–7 season in 1972 was disappointing, the same record in 1974 created reason for hope. That year, the Jets turned a 1–7 record around by winning their final six games. However, the team was not able to continue that success.

Three years after Ewbank left the sideline, Namath was gone too. Namath threw just four touchdown passes while being intercepted 16 times in 1976. He was let go after the season.

Walt Michaels took over in 1977 and coached the team through its third straight 3–11 season. The NFL expanded its schedule to 16 games the next year. The Jets made it to .500 again. They went 8–8 in both the 1978 and 1979 seasons.

The progress the team seemed to be making lost its momentum in 1980. The Jets went just 4–12. But thanks to a commitment to defense, brighter days were ahead.

CHAPTER 4

DEFENSIVE DOMINANCE

Star power shifted from the offensive to the defensive side of the ball in New York in 1981. With defensive linemen Joe Klecko and Mark Gastineau leading the way, the Jets' pass rush earned a catchy new nickname: "the New York Sack Exchange." The Sack Exchange was one of the biggest reasons for the team's first winning season, 10–5–1, since the leagues merged in 1970.

Richard Todd—like Joe Namath, a former Alabama quarterback—led the passing attack. Speedy wide receiver Wesley Walker, sturdy tight end Jerome Barkum, and all-purpose back Bruce Harper gave Todd plenty of quality targets for his passes. Todd threw for 3,231 yards and 25 touchdowns that year.

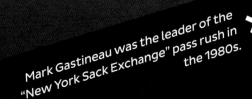

Mark Gastineau was the leader of the "New York Sack Exchange" pass rush in the 1980s.

DYNAMIC DUO

The Jets had two of the AFC's most feared defensive linemen in the 1980s. Joe Klecko made the Pro Bowl at three different positions. Klecko, a former standout at Temple University, played for the Jets from 1977 to 1987. He reached all-star status as a defensive end and a tackle in a four-man front. He was honored again after making the switch to nose tackle, the middle spot, in defensive coordinator Bud Carson's 3–4 defense.

Mark Gastineau came out of small East Central Oklahoma State University to play for the Jets from 1979 to 1988. During that time, Gastineau had plenty of opportunities to show off his celebratory dances after sacks. He led the league in sacks twice and had more than 100 in his career. Gastineau was selected as the 1984 NFL Defensive Player of the Year. His career was hampered by injuries the next few years, which contributed to his decision to retire midway through the 1988 season.

On the other side of the ball, Klecko and Gastineau combined for more than 40 sacks that year. (Unofficially—the NFL didn't make sacks an official statistic until 1982.) They were joined on the four-man defensive front by Marty Lyons and Abdul Salaam.

The Jets won seven of their final eight regular-season games to qualify for the playoffs for the first time since 1969.

✗ The Jets' Freeman McNeil (24) looks for running room against the Raiders during the AFC playoffs in January 1983.

However, they fell behind the visiting Buffalo Bills 24–0 in their AFC wild-card game. The Jets fought back but lost 31–27.

An NFL players' strike shortened the 1982 regular season to a nine-game schedule for each team. Freeman McNeil rushed for 786 yards to become the first Jet to lead the NFL in rushing yards. The Jets finished the regular season 6–3. They then reached the AFC Championship Game by beating the Cincinnati Bengals 44–17 and the Los Angeles Raiders 17–14. They fell one step short of a Super Bowl, however, losing 14–0 to the host Miami Dolphins in the AFC title game.

MUD BOWL

The AFC Championship Game after the 1982 regular season became known as the Mud Bowl. Playing in swampy conditions at the Orange Bowl in Miami, the Jets' offense could not move. New York's Freeman McNeil rushed for just 46 yards on 17 carries in the Miami mud. Forced to rely more heavily on the passing game, Richard Todd was intercepted five times. The Dolphins won 14–0, and afterwards some Jets said they suspected Dolphins coach Don Shula left the field uncovered in the rain in the days before the game to slow down the Jets' speedy offense.

Coach Walt Michaels left the Jets after the season. Offensive coordinator Joe Walton took over as coach and was unable to continue the playoff streak. New York went 7–9 in 1983. The Jets lost their final home game at Shea Stadium, 34–7 to the Pittsburgh Steelers. In 1984 they moved to Giants Stadium at the Meadowlands in northern New Jersey.

Gastineau led the league in sacks in 1983 and 1984. He set an NFL record with 22 sacks in 1984. However, he was unable to help the team avoid another 7–9 season. Jets quarterback Ken O'Brien emerged to guide a record-setting offense in 1985. On November 17 the Jets lit up the scoreboard against the Tampa Bay Buccaneers. O'Brien threw five touchdown passes,

Dolphins linebacker A. J. Duhe (77) intercepts a Richard Todd pass in the Jets' muddy AFC title game loss in Miami.

including three to tight end Mickey Shuler. The Jets had their highest-scoring game ever that day in a 62–28 win. The Jets finished 11–5 and clinched another playoff trip but lost 26–14 to visiting New England in the AFC wild-card round.

The offense got rolling again early in the 1986 season. O'Brien and Miami's Dan Marino combined for 927 passing yards, an NFL record at the time, when the host Jets beat the Dolphins 51–45 in overtime on September 21. Walker set a team record by catching four touchdown passes in the game. His 43-yard touchdown reception in overtime won it for New York.

The shootout win over the Dolphins was the first victory in a team-record nine-game winning streak by the Jets. However, Gastineau, Klecko, linebacker Lance Mehl, and tackle Reggie McElroy all suffered knee injuries that season. The team soon fell apart. New York lost its final five games to finish 10–6. Gastineau returned in time for the Jets' 35–15 wild-card playoff win over Kansas City. But New York was eliminated in the divisional round, 23–20 in double overtime at Cleveland.

The Jets slipped back below .500 in three of the next four years. The only exception, an 8–7–1 mark in 1988, was not a cause for celebration. That was the year Klecko left the team before the season because of injuries and Gastineau retired midway through the season.

The struggles continued into the early 1990s. The team changed management, coaches, and quarterbacks. However, New York was unable to produce a winning season. The best

Ken O'Brien put up some big numbers as the Jets' starting quarterback from 1985 to 1991.

the Jets could manage from 1989 through 1996 were 8–8 marks in 1991 and 1993. That was good enough to make the 1991 playoffs, but the Jets lost 17–10 to the Houston Oilers in the first round.

O'Brien was the starting quarterback through 1991, when he made the Pro Bowl. But he missed much of training camp in 1992 in a contract dispute. Then changes were made that

TRADING FOR A COACH

Bill Parcells was unhappy but still under contract with New England when the Jets tried to hire him as their general manager in 1997. The teams fought over the issue. The NFL had to get involved. During the controversy, Bill Belichick, an assistant coach on Parcells' staff with the Patriots, was going to become Jets head coach under Parcells. That plan lasted just six days, however. Parcells was named head coach, and Belichick became assistant head coach/secondary coach for the Jets.

Part of the deal allowing Parcells to move to New York was the requirement that the Jets send four draft picks, including a first-rounder, to the Patriots. Belichick left New York in 2000 and used the draft picks the Jets sent the Patriots to build a Super Bowl dynasty as New England's head coach.

eventually led to eight different quarterbacks starting for the Jets from 1992 through 1996.

The franchise hit rock bottom in the 1995 and 1996 seasons, winning just four games in two years under coach Rich Kotite. The Jets gave up 30 or more points in six of the final seven games in a miserable 1–15 season in 1996. Kotite's resignation led to the controversial pursuit of New England Patriots head coach Bill Parcells, who took over as the Jets' head coach and general manager.

Parcells made a big splash in his Jets debut. Neil O'Donnell threw five touchdown passes in a 41–3 romp over the Seattle Seahawks. New York produced its first winning season since 1988. However, at 9–7 the Jets just missed a playoff berth.

The next year was their finest season since the Super Bowl victory. The Jets went 12–4 and won their first AFC East title in 1998. Veteran Vinny Testaverde, who signed in the offseason, took over as the starting quarterback early in the season. Testaverde threw for 3,256 yards and 29 touchdowns with just seven interceptions.

On January 10, 1999, against the Jacksonville Jaguars, wide receiver Keyshawn Johnson played a huge role in the Jets' first playoff win since 1986. Johnson caught a touchdown pass in the first quarter and ran for a score in the second quarter to give the host Jets a 17–0 lead. He then preserved a 34–24 win by filling in as an extra defensive back and making a late interception. The next week, the visiting Jets led Denver 10–0 in the third quarter of the AFC Championship Game. But six turnovers—four in the second half—caught up with the Jets, and the Broncos came back for a 23–10 victory. It was the closest the Jets would come to reaching the Super Bowl for a long time.

CHAPTER 5

ROLLER COASTER

The early part of the 2000 Jets season was about comebacks. Quarterback Vinny Testaverde returned from a ruptured Achilles tendon that had cost him most of the 1999 season. His return led New York to a team-record 4–0 start.

That was just the beginning. On a Monday night game in late October, the Miami Dolphins opened a 30–7 third-quarter lead on the Jets. Then Testaverde caught fire. He ended the night with 378 passing yards and five touchdowns. Four of the touchdown passes came during a 30-point fourth quarter, including one to offensive tackle Jumbo Elliot that tied the score and forced overtime. John Hall's 40-yard field goal in overtime lifted the host Jets to a 40–37 victory.

Quarterback Vinny Testaverde had a strong comeback year in 2000.

✕ Jets running back Curtis Martin led the NFL with 1,697 rushing yards in 2004.

The game became known as "the Monday Night Miracle." The win gave New York a 6–1 start. Unfortunately for the Jets, the season ended in disappointment as they finished 9–7.

The Jets made it to the playoffs five times in the 2000s, the most in any decade in team history. But ultimately they all ended in frustration. In 2001 as wild cards and in 2002 as the AFC East champions, the Jets were knocked out of the playoffs by their old AFL rivals in Oakland.

The 2004 team finished the season with three straight overtime games. New York lost to the St. Louis Rams 32–29 in overtime to end a 10–6 season. The Jets then defeated the San Diego Chargers 20–17 in overtime in the wild-card round before falling to the Pittsburgh Steelers 20–17 in the divisional round, also in overtime.

The 2006 team's big finish to the regular season included a 23–3 New Year's Eve triumph over Oakland to clinch a playoff berth. The New England Patriots were too much for the Jets while running away for a 37–16 win in the wild-card round the next week. After winning five straight games in 2008 to reach 8–3, the Jets lost four of their final five and missed the playoffs in Hall of Fame quarterback Brett Favre's lone season in New York.

The next year, the Jets replaced Favre with rookie Mark Sanchez. Sanchez was a first-round draft pick from the University of Southern California. He was supported by the

✕ Mark Sanchez quarterbacked the Jets to the AFC Championship Game in each of his first two years as a starter.

NFL's top running game and defense. A late surge put the Jets in the playoffs, where they rattled off road wins in Cincinnati and San Diego. Then the Jets took a 17–6 lead in the AFC Championship Game in Indianapolis. But their luck ran out there, as Peyton Manning led the Colts back to a 30–17 win.

New York used a similar formula in 2010. The Jets finished the season a strong 11–5 but could not jump ahead of the rival Patriots for the AFC East championship. Sanchez and the Jets entered the playoffs as a wild card. They went on the road and got revenge on the Colts, as Nick Folk's 32-yard field goal at the gun gave them a 17–16 win.

The next week, New York had a game for the ages at New England. After telling the media all week they could defeat the powerful Patriots, the Jets did just that. New York's defense did a lot of the work as they forced star quarterback Tom Brady to throw his first interception since Week 6 of the regular season. The Jets, who were nine-point underdogs, also sacked Brady five times in a 28–21 win.

Once again, however, New York lost in the AFC Championship Game. The Jets fell behind the Steelers 24–0 in Pittsburgh, and a furious second-half rally wasn't enough to prevent a 24–19 defeat.

That was the last the Jets would see of the postseason for a long time. From 2011 to 2018, New York finished above

BACK-END BLUNDER

The Jets had a big game on Thanksgiving in 2012. They were at home facing the rival Patriots. New York needed a win to stay in the playoff hunt. But the game turned out to be memorable for all the wrong reasons. In the second quarter, Jets quarterback Mark Sanchez took the snap. He ran with the ball and collided with teammate Brandon Moore's backside. Sanchez fumbled, and New England returned it for a touchdown in a 49–19 rout of the Jets. The play came to be known as the "Butt Fumble" and was a symbol of Sanchez's numerous struggles with the Jets.

.500 only once. Sanchez struggled to repeat his success after making the AFC Championship Game in each of his first two years. Looking to make a change, the Jets drafted University of West Virginia quarterback Geno Smith in the second round of the 2013 NFL Draft. But Smith lasted only four seasons with the Jets, failing to live up to his potential. He threw 28 touchdown passes and 36 interceptions with the Jets.

In the midst of this losing, head coach Rex Ryan was let go after the 2014 season. New York went with another defensive coach in Todd Bowles. He was successful in his first season behind quarterback Ryan Fitzpatrick and running back Chris Ivory. The Jets had the league's eleventh-ranked scoring offense and gave up the ninth-fewest points in the NFL. They finished 10–6 and came up just short of the playoffs after a loss to the Buffalo Bills on the final day of the season.

But Bowles could not get the team above .500 during the next three seasons and lost his job after going 4–12 in 2018. The Jets played that season with rookie Sam Darnold under center. Darnold was the third pick in the 2018 NFL Draft, and though the team struggled, the young quarterback had some promising moments. For instance, in consecutive losses to Houston and Green Bay in late December, Darnold completed 48 of 73 passes for 594 yards with five touchdown passes and

✕ Quarterback Sam Darnold (14) had a promising rookie season for the Jets in 2018.

no interceptions. It was the type of performance that showed why he was drafted so high. In January 2019 the team hired Adam Gase, a longtime NFL offensive assistant who also served as head coach of the Miami Dolphins, as its new head coach. Jets fans hoped Gase and Darnold could join forces and send the team back to the Super Bowl.

TIMELINE

Harry Wismer is granted a franchise, the New York Titans, in the AFL's first organizational meeting in Chicago on August 14.

The Titans win their debut 27–3 over the Buffalo Bills before 10,200 people (only 5,727 paid) on a rainy day at the Polo Grounds in New York on September 11.

The franchise's new ownership group announces the change in name from Titans to Jets and hires future Hall of Famer Weeb Ewbank as coach on April 15.

The Jets move into their new home, Shea Stadium, and defeat the Denver Broncos 30–6 on September 12.

Quarterback Joe Namath, the team's first-round draft pick, signs with the Jets on January 2 for what is then the largest contract in pro football history.

1959

1960

1963

1964

1965

Namath becomes the first player in pro football history to throw for 4,000 yards in a season.

The Jets beat the Oakland Raiders 27–23 on December 29 to win the AFL Championship.

Namath is named Super Bowl MVP after leading the Jets to a 16–7 victory over the Baltimore Colts on January 12.

The Jets make their NFL debut in the first *Monday Night Football* game on ABC-TV, a 31–21 loss to the Cleveland Browns on September 21.

Namath completes 15 of 28 passes for 496 yards and six touchdowns in a 44–34 win over the Colts on September 24.

1967

1968

1969

1970

1972

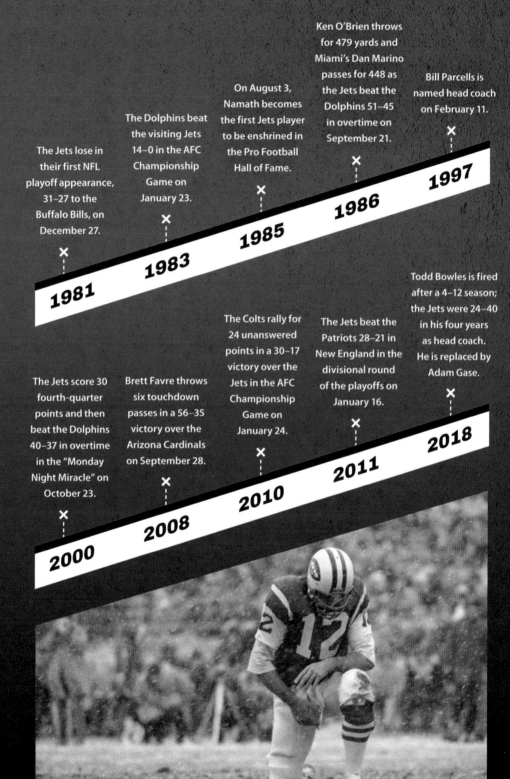

The Jets lose in their first NFL playoff appearance, 31–27 to the Buffalo Bills, on December 27.

✗

1981

The Dolphins beat the visiting Jets 14–0 in the AFC Championship Game on January 23.

✗

1983

On August 3, Namath becomes the first Jets player to be enshrined in the Pro Football Hall of Fame.

✗

1985

Ken O'Brien throws for 479 yards and Miami's Dan Marino passes for 448 as the Jets beat the Dolphins 51–45 in overtime on September 21.

✗

1986

Bill Parcells is named head coach on February 11.

✗

1997

The Jets score 30 fourth-quarter points and then beat the Dolphins 40–37 in overtime in the "Monday Night Miracle" on October 23.

✗

2000

Brett Favre throws six touchdown passes in a 56–35 victory over the Arizona Cardinals on September 28.

✗

2008

The Colts rally for 24 unanswered points in a 30–17 victory over the Jets in the AFC Championship Game on January 24.

✗

2010

The Jets beat the Patriots 28–21 in New England in the divisional round of the playoffs on January 16.

✗

2011

Todd Bowles is fired after a 4–12 season; the Jets were 24–40 in his four years as head coach. He is replaced by Adam Gase.

✗

2018

QUICK STATS

FRANCHISE HISTORY

New York Titans, 1960–62 (AFL)
New York Jets, 1963–69 (AFL)
New York Jets, 1970– (NFL)

SUPER BOWLS
(wins in bold)

1968 (III)

AFL CHAMPIONSHIP GAMES *(1960–69, wins in bold)*

1968

AFC CHAMPIONSHIP GAMES *(since 1970 AFL-NFL merger)*

1982, 1998, 2009, 2010

DIVISION CHAMPIONSHIPS *(since 1970 AFL-NFL merger)*

1998, 2002

KEY COACHES

Weeb Ewbank (1963–73): 71–77–6, 2–1 (playoffs)
Bill Parcells (1997–99): 29–19, 1–1 (playoffs)
Rex Ryan (2009–14): 46–50, 4–2 (playoffs)

KEY PLAYERS
(position, seasons with team)

Wayne Chrebet (WR, 1995–2005)
Mark Gastineau (DE, 1979–88)
David Harris (LB, 2007–16)
Joe Klecko (DT/DE, 1977–87)
Pat Leahy (K, 1974–91)
Mo Lewis (LB, 1991–2003)
Curtis Martin (RB, 1998–2005)
Kevin Mawae (C, 1998–2005)
Don Maynard (WR, 1960–72)
Freeman McNeil (RB, 1981–92)
Joe Namath (QB, 1965–76)
Ken O'Brien (QB, 1984–92)
Darrelle Revis (CB, 2007–12, 2015–16)
Matt Snell (FB, 1964–72)
Richard Todd (QB, 1976–83)
Al Toon (WR, 1985–92)
Wesley Walker (WR, 1977–89)
Muhammad Wilkerson (DT, 2011–17)

HOME FIELDS

MetLife Stadium (2010–)
Giants Stadium (1984–2009)
Shea Stadium (1964–83)
Polo Grounds (1960–63)

* All statistics through 2018 season

QUOTES AND ANECDOTES

New York Jets quarterback Richard Todd and fullback Clark Gaines put up record-setting numbers in a losing effort on September 21, 1980. Todd set an NFL record for completions in a game. The mark has since been broken. Todd completed 42 of 60 pass attempts for 447 yards and three touchdowns in a 37–27 loss to the San Francisco 49ers. Gaines caught 17 passes. That remained the team record through 2018.

The Jets were not always comfortable at Shea Stadium, their home field for two decades. A team statement announcing the move to Giants Stadium in East Rutherford, New Jersey, in 1983 summed up those feelings. In the release, the Jets described Shea Stadium as "rundown, neglected, and the NFL's poorest facility for athletes and spectators alike."

The kelly green in the Jets' uniform colors is the same as the color used at Hess gas stations. Leon Hess owned at least part of the team from 1963 until his death in 1999.

On April 15, 2000, the Jets became the first team to make four selections in the first round of an NFL Draft. They took defensive end Shaun Ellis twelfth, defensive end John Abraham thirteenth, quarterback Chad Pennington eighteenth, and tight end Anthony Becht twenty-seventh.

The Jets have played in only one Super Bowl, but they did win in their one opportunity. As of 2018, they are one of three NFL teams to win their lone Super Bowl appearance. The other two teams are the New Orleans Saints and Tampa Bay Buccaneers.

GLOSSARY

bankrupt
Financially ruined; a company or person who has less money and assets than money owed.

berth
A place, spot, or position, such as in the NFL playoffs.

comeback
When a team losing a game rallies to tie the score or take the lead.

contract
An agreement to play for a certain team.

draft
A system that allows teams to acquire new players coming into a league.

franchise
A sports organization, including the top-level team and all minor

guarantee
A promise that something will definitely happen.

merge
Join with another to create something new, such as a company, a team, or a league.

retire
To end one's career.

rookie
A professional athlete in his or her first year of competition.

rupture
The act of breaking or bursting.

wild card
A team that makes the playoffs even though it did not win its division.

MORE INFORMATION

BOOKS

Blumberg, Saulie. *New York Jets*. Minneapolis, MN: Abdo Publishing, 2017.

Donnelly, Patrick. *Joe Namath's Super Bowl Guarantee*. Minneapolis, MN: Abdo Publishing, 2015.

Zappa, Marcia. *New York Jets*. Minneapolis, MN: Abdo Publishing, 2015.

ONLINE RESOURCES

To learn more about the New York Jets, visit **abdobooklinks.com** or scan this QR code. These links are routinely monitored and updated to provide the most current information available.

PLACE TO VISIT

The Atlantic Health Jets Training Center
1 Jets Drive
Florham Park, NJ 07932
973–549–4844
newyorkjets.com/faqs/training-camp-faq

This facility hosts the team's training camp each season. It opened in 2008.

INDEX

ABOUT THE AUTHOR

Todd Ryan is a library assistant from the Upper Peninsula of Michigan. He lives near Houghton with his two cats, Izzo and Mooch.